Awakening

Richard Harries

Stairwell Books //

Published by Stairwell Books
161 Lowther Street
York, YO31 7LZ

www.stairwellbooks.co.uk
@stairwellbooks

ISBN: 978-1-913432-24-9

Layout design: Alan Gillott

Cover art: Jim Danby

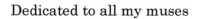

Dedicated to all my muses

Table of Contents

Awakening

The vast stone woke up
From its sleep of a million years
It felt deep inside itself
Down to its inner core
Deep into the earth
To the centre of the planet
It looked outwards down the steep hillside
At the world, which had changed
Since it had last been awake
Then the planet had been verdant
Fresh, pure
Creatures of all kinds had existed
Giant lumbering beasts, small animals
Birds and insects
All surviving and leaving no imprint
No destruction no sign of their lives

Now the stone, the spirit of the earth
Viewed with dismay the destruction of the planet
Creatures on two legs walked, ran, existed
Behind them they left things
Mess, litter, destruction
Translucent things were on the ground and in the oceans
Things that looked as though they would be there for
thousands of years
Violation of the planet everywhere
Grasslands covered, forests destroyed
Smoke, pollution
Everywhere so unnatural
The stone felt it should fight back
And it knew how it should
It could raise a volcano
Cause reaction the planet over
Destroy these creatures
Let the planet recover from them

But then it thought deep
And went back to sleep
Believing it could wake again
In a million years
And the destructive two legs would be gone, forgotten
Having destroyed themselves. Completely ⁄⁄

Benefits Scrounger

Esme was a cleaner
A grafter, not well paid
Became ill, could not breath easily
Went to her doctor, treatment did not help
Referred her to the chest clinic, all this time on sick leave
Lots of tests on vastly expensive machines
Diagnosed by a specialist, a great man in his field
Chronic Obstructive Airways Disease

I went to see her, applied for DLA
I was warned to wait at the door
Took Esme 10 minutes to get there
Holding onto the wall, slowly, gasping, moving
Back to her chair, oxygen by her side,
She used it all the time if she ever went out, which was
rare
Her husband carried the cylinder, too heavy for her
DLA form submitted

Doctor from Benefits Agency attended to assess
To her face called her a Benefits Scrounger
DLA refused
Statements from husband and GP ignored
Submitted review, with more statements
Including the specialists, all supporting Esme
Within my letter gave notice of appeal
Stated that if review failed
Said I would ambulance Esme to a tribunal
On camera and if possible on TV

Review allowed, payment backdated
That was not important,
Esme wanted to be believed, Esme delighted
I complained about the doctor, formally
'To be retrained' they said. Not sacked. No apology
10 months later Esme

The woman who could not breathe
That benefits scrounger ... died
The doctor? No doubt still
Earning his money on top of his GP wedge
For a bit of overtime

Now whom would YOU call
A Benefits Scrounger? ⚆

A Tale of Warning for Men

A true story from my time at an Advice Centre with names changed

Went to the doctor's last Christmas
For something else, some minor condition
But mentioned while I was there
I had a sore nipple, no idea why
Had not hurt myself, that I could remember
Just mentioned it, I was not worried, could see alarm on
his face
And I found myself within days
At Cottingham, at the breast cancer clinic
Seems this is a common sign
That there could be a real problem
The problem, the problem that has killed so many

I sat there with my wife and felt strange
Many women there mostly with their husbands
Mostly young. I felt weird and bewildered
Uneasy, Terrified, Alone, the only man with this problem
Until they started to call out the patient's names
Several were men, not the wives
I was not alone and not unusual
I was the only man though who was not a young lad
With decades in front of them, they all seemed so fit
And glowing with health
It seems this for men is not uncommon
Yet it's something that men do not think about
Breast cancer affecting them

Went for the mammogram
The nurse said I would have been warned by the wife
Warned? No I've come for like a photograph!
An X-ray type thing. Wrong!
They grab, and twist, and stretch and clamp
Yes! Clamp in metal, then they photograph
As they grab your shoulders and manoeuvre you
It's bloody painful and women don't tell you about it
Maybe cos they don't think you'll want to know

5

Or maybe cos it's a bad memory but I'm telling you
Cos you should know, you must know
It's scary, they stick a needle into your nipple and take
tissue
Then they examine you and ask if the nipple is sore
It was before but by now it's bloody sore
They ask if you noticed a difference in your nipple
I never looked, but I should and now you should too
They said they thought all was okay, felt good
But then a letter of recall and they do the tests again
It's a nightmare BUT finally, the all clear. Thank God ⁄⁄

Tragedy at Flamborough, 1952

I look back through the mists of time
Into my memory, my childhood
To a day that affected and moved me
All my life
I was at the seaside
In Flamborough, on holiday
That dreadful day in 1952
When two girls went swimming
So happy shrieking with laughter
To me they seemed so old, so grand
As teenagers do when you are five

There were winds
And the sea was rough, so rough
The girls were swept out as we watched
Crowds gathering, hoping, praying

The Flamborough Lifeboat could not launch
I am told there were repairs
Being done to the slipway
So ropes were fired and one of girls
Reached the rope but could not hold on
Gillian and Joan were their names
That day of horror in 1952

The Bridlington lifeboat had been launched
The crowds on the cliffs watched and shouted
And those brave men fought to save the lives
Of the teenage girls, they found one but it was too late
As they entered Thornwick Bay they were hit by a wave
Rolled over, capsized and five men, valiant brave men
Fell into the sea

They were swept towards shore and some made it there
But the bowman, who had clung to the stern
Drowned. A valiant father of three

The second girl's body was found a week later

Sadness and tragedy enveloped Flamborough
That terrible day
It enveloped me
It affected me so much
And always will ⧄

Dedicated to Marian Bean who witnessed this event as a small child

Naked Evil

In Osset the rain was pouring down
There was no pleasure staying there
We rushed to the car and thought of where to go
Birstall or Morley seemed the places most likely
And on the horizon saw blue sky
So drove that way to escape the rain
As we went towards this lightness
It became apparent to Morley we would go
Our old home town
And when we got there it was sunny and dry
So off we went had a coffee
And then a walk round the town

Into a community charity shop we went
I saw a china angel on a shelf behind the till
But could not get the attention of the shopkeeper
Was about to get annoyed when she started to cry
Stood still in shock. 'Jo Cox has been shot' she said

She had the radio on and it had just announced
The murder of a well-loved local MP
In the street in Birstall, where we had nearly gone
That afternoon
Her shock and trauma were complete
Then an old woman also in the shop
Snarled and shouted 'Immigrants again'
I looked amazed and told her
The radio had said it was a local man
'Nothing bad ever happened here till these immigrants
came'
Said the evil old bag in a rage
'So the Yorkshire Ripper was foreign was he
And the Black Panther too?' I said
She snarled and shouted 'You'll get yours Karma's coming
for you
For sympathising with them', spouting her evil and hate

She announced that when Brexit was voted in
We could get rid of all immigrants and crime

I was shocked by the murder in a place so familiar and
near
And shocked by the hate and unjust blame handed out
And saw evil, naked evil looking so ordinary
And so vile ⁄⁄

My Luck

Had my hip replaced
Was in pain afterwards for a while
Looked after in hospital
Brought home by ambulance
Helped inside my home
My wife nursed me, brilliantly
Missed having a bath
But after washing well for a while
Had a glorious hot shower
Power shower, felt great
Got some pain in my joints
Used heat pads, deep heat spray
My eczema had returned
Annoying but have emollient creams
Had extra showers and soothed the itching
All under control
If uncomfortable, more hot showers
Snuggled down in my bed, thick duvets
Warm, can rest and recover, lucky me
Pain gone, recovered well

But what if I was homeless?
What if I was not lucky?
Can you imagine the misery?
Pain and depression of being ill
Needing help
And lying out, vulnerable to attack
While the Christmas shoppers go by?
How in the name of humanity can we allow
This suffering on our wealthy streets
And a suffering that is growing
Is not being addressed and not reduced
How? //

A Lesson Learnt

As a child I did what I was told
Back then you did
But when I was ten
I was watching TV
Together with my family
As you did back then
Tennis was on, Wimbledon
My Mum liked Maria Bueno
Said she was elegant
Pretty, had class

A match was starting
Women's tennis
On walked a short woman
Not glamorous, not wearing lace
Like Maria Bueno
She walked on determinedly, defiantly
Wearing colour
Only a wristband or something like that

A first at Wimbledon
Rosie Casals
It caused a fuss, shock, horror
She was sent off to change
She was timed
Something stirred in me
I learnt I could disobey, I could protest
Did not have to accept

Thank you Rosie Casals ⁄⁄

Five Strong Women

I was left without a mother when young
But that is not what I want to talk about
When that happened I found strength
Hope, love, life
From five amazing women
They each stood up to be counted
And helped and carried me on my way
They chose to do this

My life became richer, deeper, vibrant
Bearable because of these women
Who CHOSE to love and help
And advise and support me
All in so many different ways
They travelled to see me
Wrote, loved, baked cakes
Gave me shelter, several homes
Talked to me, planned with me

Loved me

I won't tell each of their stories
And they are now all gone
Grieved for and mourned
But I loved them all
And they amazingly loved me
For that my gratitude and love
Eternal will be

Bless ⁄⁄

Afternoon Delight

1967, a trip to the record shop
Two Motown singles to love forever more
Martha and her Vandellas stomping out 'Jimmy Mack'
Brenda Holloway telling us 'Just look What You Done'
I was 14, my sister 18
At those ages siblings don't mix
But our toes started tapping
And for a joyous afternoon
We played these tracks and their flips
Over and over and over and then over again
Brenda 'Starting the hurt all over again'
And Martha and the girls proclaiming
That third finger left hand
Was where he placed the wedding band
We danced so much, we laughed a lot
We made four dance routines, one for each track
So glad we did not have mobile phones
Or any means to capture those moves

But even now when the tracks come on
And in my house they do
My toes start tapping, I wear a smile
And my mind floods with happy memories
My sister died many years ago
And that afternoon was so special
So full of joy
The routines?
Well I reckon I could still, at a push
Dance out the one for Jimmy Mack!
But not with a camera or a mobile phone around! ∥

I Grew Up in Harrogate

I grew up in Harrogate
Affluent, my Dad was rich
A director of ICI
I went to Ashville College, a boarder
Though my home was in town I boarded

My mother died
Then within weeks a stepmother arrived
So fast, I was hurting still
Bewildered, time passed
And I was not welcome home
Homeless in the holidays
So I went to friends and relatives
Stayed with them, but then I left school
Grew up, stayed with my sister for a while
But then the time came to leave
Stand alone, Dad was now in Belgium
I was not welcome, got jobs
In bars and hotels

Moved into a bed sit on Stray Rein
It was dirty, lonely, awful
An old woman rented a room
Not a home to me
Not allowed to see her telly
Or sit and speak with her
Her dog shit in the bath
For which she charged ten shillings extra
The bath, not the faeces
She was not surprised when I complained
The final straw was when she made me a coffee
(breakfast was included)
There was a dead spider floating on the top
She neither saw it nor cared

I gave notice and she tried to screw me
For an extra month's rent
Even though she knew I had nothing
And worked in a bar
It was a dreadful start to my life as an adult
I left school looking to the future
Excited, then this:
I grew up in Harrogate ⁄⁄

Originally published in part in the Haunt Anthology (Imove, 2015).

Alone in Harrogate Town

I was pregnant, homeless, often drunk
This was the sixties, meant to be swinging
Sandie Shaw and Petula Clark
Did not live like me
I was judged, despised, called a tart
Lived with friends
On their couches, on their floors
Stayed in Harrogate
Stayed in Knaresborough
Wherever I could
Whoever would have me
I used to stand on the steps of the Alex
Near the posh cenotaph, near Montpelier
Near Austin Reed
Where my dad shopped for clothes
I was short and blond
Folk said I was like
Sweet Hayley Mills
Another part of the sixties
That for me did not swing
I held a pint in my hand
Men would look amazed
Say daft things like
'Big drink for a little girl'
Girl! I was 20!
'Bet you a pint I can drink it in one' I'd say
They took me up on it
I supped it fast
Got my next drink and so it went on
Then I'd wake up
In a strange bed
With someone I did not know
My dad? When I got pregnant his help offered?
100 quid to change my name by deed poll
Before my baby arrived
She was born in Harrogate Hospital

One night and I was alone
When she came I loved her but I did not get to keep her
I gave up my baby, I had no place to call home
She was adopted, gone
I carried on. No home to call my home
I never had another baby and I never had a home
In Harrogate, that fine town ⁄⁄

In memory of my late sister Judi (Judith) Fairclough (née Harries) originally published in the Haunt Anthology (Imove, 2015)

Oh What Joy!

When I was 19 started a job
The older guys working there seemed ancient
They were, I think, around 50
So very, very old, dressed old, acted old
Old in mind it seemed to me
I was happy to be young
To be married, to start a family

Then I found more joy
I got to 30
Happy to be there
Time passed and I got to 40
More joy indeed
Time kept flying and I was 50
Yes I got to 50
Joy, such joy, so lucky, so glad

Then astonishingly I got to 60
Joy abounded with amazement
How could that be?
When did this happen?
And so fast
So happy and joyous to be there

I had arrived at 60
Oh no that can't be
But happily I never grew up
Really act quite disreputably
I hope
And am not seen as ancient by the young
I hope, oh I so hope

Now I am heading very fast to seventy
Am well past the halfway stage
And am full of joy
And fun
And know I am lucky
Lucky just to be
Thankfully full of joy
As full as can be ⁄⁄

So Easy to Gamble

Gambling amongst the young is growing
Casinos online
So much growth of this on the internet
New ways
So easy to access
Poker for the young
All has been normalised
The generation that just grew up
Is the first to see gambling
As usual, everyday
Before it was somehow seedy
The sort of thing your uncle did
On a Saturday, behind closed doors
Doors he hesitated at
And looked all around before he went in

Now it's advertised on the telly
On footballers tops
Gambling stats rise dramatically
Yet Smoking ads are banned
And smoking amongst the young declines
Gambling addiction is a problem
A disease that destroys life
Relationships
Causes misery and devastation

Why is this allowed to go unchecked?
Why is it so heavily promoted?
And easily accessible?
It can't just be
Because very wealthy and powerful
People with the Government's ear
Get even wealthier
Because of it
And it generates millions
In taxation
Can it? ⁄⁄

On the Edge

He climbed onto the ledge of the parapet
The one he had chosen, so carefully
Beforehand
He moved slowly forward
And stood on the edge
Looked down so far, so very far
He could see people, tiny like ants

He would have to wait for quiet
Did not want to hurt people
When he fell and landed
Felt battered, bruised, labelled, despised
Bullied, ignored, isolated, lachrymose

He was not human
Not really
No rights of his own
He had had hopes
That had been crushed
Slowly, repeatedly, inexorably
Personally and professionally
Closing in on him
Till he could bear it no more

His stomach churned
He felt panic in his heart
And gut, and mind, and soul

Despair, and no wish to go on
So low, aware of the waste
Yet he could not go on
No more pain, ejection
He was done
The time had come

And then, he heard the sound
Of footsteps approach
Help was coming
Voices talking soft
Reassuring words of encouragement

So, he jumped ⫽

Dealing With It

I will deal with it
Deal with it
Deal with it
I will deal with it

All my life I have said this
Said it out loud and in my head
I have felt it
Hurt it
I have dealt with it

Lies and hate and derision
Non acceptance, slights and Losses

I have dealt with it
Dealt with it
Dealt with it
Dealt with it
I have dealt with it indeed

I have survived
Bereavement, unemployment
Uncertainty, being let down
It made me strong

I am not a survivor
I am a thriver
I have dealt with it
Dealt with it
Dealt with it
I moved on

I have had liars
Control freaks
And alcoholics in my life
And I dealt with it
And moved on

Now I am older, not yet old
And I still deal with it
Deal with it
Deal with it
And will always move right on! ⟍

Inspired by a song written by my friend Sam Bishop

Still Missed, Occasionally

Beige
A bit worn, thread bear and scruffy
One eye sewn back on
A loose ear stitched back on with love
She was mine
My Minnie, yes Minnie the Pooh
Cos she was a girl and not yellow
She never got stuck in a hole
I carried her
Cuddled her, loved her
Eventually she stopped being in my bed
But sat regally
I thought
On the window sill
Fading even more in the sun

I keep seeing folk on TV shows
With treasured bears they kept all their lives
Loving them, having them restored
Some getting them valued they are so old

Mine?
Sadly burnt on a bonfire
By my stepmother
She did not like me
So burnt everything I owned
Managed to keep some clothes
And thankfully my records
But left home with nothing else
It's a long time ago but I still
Occasionally, just occasionally
Miss my Minnie the Pooh //

Marie Antoinette

At 14
Traded from her home
Married off from her country
Sent alone abroad
One of the youngest
Of the many children
Of the Empress Maria Theresa
Born Maria Antonia
A Grand Duchess
They changed her name
Frenchified it
To Marie Antoinette

She bore four children
To her King
Two of whom died
She was a loving mother
But a flawed woman
Greed, arrogance
And, yes, stupidity were hers
But she was brought to live at Versailles
Surrounded by such
Golden, extravagant splendour
Luxury
Which had stretched back
Through the years to the Sun King
Why would she not spend?

She was hated as 'the Austrian Woman'
Yet all princesses were bartered off
In marriage abroad
How she spent and wasted
Was outrageous and the poor did suffer
But her final journey in a wooden cart
Following her husband Louis
To death in public

By guillotine
Was wicked

But then so many deaths
In the Terror that followed were wicked
And greedy power-hungry
Men and woman replaced the old corrupt court
She died with composure, with dignity

Have we learnt from history?
Surely no politician now
Would spend millions on palaces or seats of Government
While citizens starved, went homeless and queued at Food
Banks

Would they? ⁄⁄

Modern Slavery

William Wilberforce
From Hull
Fought slavery
As did many others
He thought and they thought
The fight was won
As it should be

But human greed
And desire for power
And control
Was not ended
Not eradicated
So a different form of slavery was born
Into the modern world

Not based on race but based on profit
From the prostitutes of Turin
Forced to work having fled from Africa
In search of a better life
To the cockle workers
In Morecambe Bay, whose deaths
Highlighted the tragedies
Of modern slavery

Gender, debt, childhood
All can be exploited by the evil
Used for control and profit
Refugee or immigrant status too
As many are forced to work
In domestic servitude
Forced marriage too
These iniquitous practices continue
They thrive disgracing humanity
Hard work and vigilance
Resistance, rescue and complaint

Against this power and greed
Is the way to stop
This dreadful practise ⁄⁄

Eileen and Her Memory

Now Eileen has a memory
A formidable memory
An accurate far-reaching memory
And we have been together many years
Yes many years, in fact 47

The other day I finished a jar of pickled onions
Yes I did
I like pickled onions
Petula likes pickled onions
Yes she said so in 1963
Still to this day
Fans bring jars to concerts
For her
She probably regrets making that comment
Like I regret things I said
So long ago
Remember Eileen has that accurate memory

I emptied the vinegar from the pickled onions
Into the vinegar bottle
Eileen stood still in shock
Yes she did
Shock
She looked at me

'Oh My God, it's happened'
'What has?'
'It's happened' she said again
Stunned
'What has?'
I demanded
'You
You
You
You've

Turned
Into my mother!'
'Into your MOTHER?
Me?
Oh no that can't be!
It's meant to be YOU that looks in to a mirror and sees her
not me!'
'In 1976 you said to her...'
(Eh? I SAID to her I can barely remember 1976 never mind
what I SAID!)
'You said to her that she was a mean old bugger
Re-using old onion vinegar
You called her tight
And disgusting
Complained it tasted of old onions
Sad you could NEVER eat that,
And now YOU'VE done it'.

Then she said 'I rest my case!' ⁄⁄

*As a lifelong (well since the age of four) Petula Clark fan, she does come into my
poems occasionally*

Enid Blyton Today

If Julian, Dick, Anne and George
But not Timmy the dog
Had had mobile phones
With them to use, fully charged of course
What would Enid Blyton have done?
Her books would have been short indeed
'Hey Inspector we have found bank robbers
Fraudsters / Jewel Thieves / Kidnappers
Come and arrest them fast, oh and rescue us'

And the Inspector did
Very fast, not a long book
Not even a short story
Glad Enid is not writing today
Oh! hang on
With no police on duty
And so many police station closed, demolished and sold
They may still have to do it alone

And perhaps even make their own citizens arrests ⁄⁄

And Then She Walked Away

I went for a walk feeling happy, contented
Who did I meet but her?
In a moment, in a nervous smile
Dawning of recognition
I am back returned 25 years
In an instant
We loved, deep love
Complete, declared it
Touched, caressed
And so much more
We knew each other intimately
Physically, bonding deeply
And it was forever
Till she walked away

We said nothing now
Well, spoke words
Platitudes
But they meant nothing
How could this be?
We had talked into the night
And past dawn about everything
Including our future
Together, forever
It was going to be undying love
Nothing would or could part us
We were special
I wanted to ask why?
But no deep words came
But before she walked away

I looked and saw
A ring
A ring on her wedding finger
Something she would not wear for me
Then she told me about her kids

The ones she would not have with me
I told her about my life
Happy and full
And then she walked away
Again ⁄⁄

Memories Come Flooding Back

Memories come flooding back
As I travel on a railway track
To Kings Cross Station old and fine
They brought back history that is mine
When I was eight I travelled there alone
As my travel skills I did hone
My beloved Uncle John met me there
About me I knew he did care
When I got to be eleven
I felt nervous but in heaven
And was so proud
To be allowed
To change trains just me
And go to London Bridge, feel free

So today the memories of a lovely man
As only sweet childhood memories can
Came flooding happily back
And the surprising sweetness of them did me attack
I remember well he was the first to take me to a pub
And oft with cash he did me sub
He wanted me to write
He knew I had language in sight
I was so touched when I saw his room
A school picture of me did loom
He was one of the first people who I knew really loved me
His love was unconditional and free
So I am glad I thought of him today
He long ago passed away
But in my childhood memories he is a golden ray

Slum Dwellers

They lived in an old cobbled Victorian street
A slum others called it, they thought it was sweet
They were told the new high rises built in '62
Were great, all modern with kitchens clean and new
They all had bathrooms and toilets inside
They did not have to walk to a yard outside
They left their fine community then and went
To the concrete jungle where they had been sent

At first all seemed fine with pathways high and wide
But these became rat runs where druggies could hide
They found that the flats were noisy and damp
With stolen cars abandoned on the ground floor ramp
They were told that these would be 'gardens in the sky'
Without any facilities they were left high and dry
They lived in misery, noise and fear
And in the lift area, kids faeces did smear

The whole place was messy and vandalised
They could not find the 'gardens in the skies'
It took them 15 long years to get out
After they had had to plead, beg and shout
They found that their slum street was still there
And moved back into a home which was near
To the one they had left so many years past
They found happiness and fresh air at last

By now the Victorian street had been changed
The yards for inside toilets had been exchanged
The street was happy and a community alive
And they did live well and happily thrive
The flats, which had been so new in '62
Lasted all of 20 years till they fell through
They were demolished at a huge cost
And quality of life had been totally lost

The architects had thrived and made plenty of money
But lives had been destroyed here, it wasn't funny
What I want to know is when there was blame
How no person responsible seemed to have a name? ⟋

Part of the story of the couple written about in LUCY MY LOVELY, again from my time at the advice centre, with names changed

Lucy My Lovely

She went to the Palais in '52
She had no troubles had never been blue
She was used to poverty that is true
And went to dance her cares away
But she danced herself into danger
When she met a charismatic stranger
With dark good looks and an electric touch
She found herself with him far too much

Lily my lovely I love you
And to you I'll always be true
I'll carry you, support you
And never beat you black and blue

She was a virgin, well you were then
But he made love to her again and again
She had his child so she married him then
And he beat her senseless again and again
She kept a working in Burton's factory
And life was miserable and unsatisfactory
She got pregnant again and again
She wanted to escape and wondered when

Lily my lovely I love you
And to you I'll always be true
I'll carry you, support you
And never beat you black and blue

The bane of her life was her man
Who drank, thieved and gambled
As amoral true degenerates can
She was destroyed, her brains scrambled
When salvation came when she found him
In bed with another man, a scene so grim
In '52 that was a ticket to a prison cell
So she was able to escape from her hell

Lily my lovely I love you
And to you I'll always be true
I'll carry you, support you
And never beat you black and blue

She was petite only four foot nine
With lovely hair blond and ever so fine
She was walking down the street
When a tall young stud laid love at her feet
He said he's always loved her
But he was 20 years younger
6 foot two and eyes of brown
A sunny smile, never a frown

Lily my lovely I love you
And to you I'll always be true
I'll carry you, support you
And never beat you black and blue

How could she trust a man now?
How could she believe another vow?
The lad's mother called her a slut
She caused the neighbours to frown and tut
The mother offered to buy him a house
If he would leave Lily like a louse

He arranged for her to get her divorce
Another scandal back then of course
They married and lived long in their sweet domestic bliss
Even though in the street she was greeted with many a
hiss
But when he was only 59 her giant fell mortally ill
And she nursed him faithfully as a true love will
She felt it was not the way life should be
Losing her love meant she could never be free

Lily my lovely I love you
And to you I'll always be true
I'll carry you, support you
And never beat you black and blue

She struggled on, she was 82
And time passed, never flew
When she passed away so old and grey
She knew with her giant she'd be every day
She's had a life so full and true
And happy that the love of her life she knew
And the young girl who had so dangerously danced
Had lived eventually to find romance

Lily my lovely I love you
And to you I'll always be true
I'll carry you, support you
And never beat you black and blue ⁄⁄

Desire and Temptation

By the interval temptation had entered our minds
As we thought of what was to come
In our hotel bedroom, later on
As we sat there
We felt a desire
So urgent
A hunger
That would have to be assuaged
After saying farewells to friends
There was a brief pause
To decide really what it was we wanted to do
Did we really need to?
So extreme was this, not for us usual at all
But we wanted it, needed it, urgently now!
In the car on the way to the hotel
Eileen felt heat in her lap
Real desire was there
We ran up the stairs like kids
Giggling, naughty, so full of urgent desire
Eileen stripped off right away
Put on her red silk nightie
She said she did not want to stain her clothes
I said that we should be careful, go-slow
Then all of a sudden we were both tearing away feverishly
Urgently, hungrily
Ripping noises abounded as we exposed glistening flesh
And then we greedily devoured
The first kebabs we bought in years!

Mine with the addition of chilli sauce! ⁄⁄

Three Sisters

It was an innocent time
Three young ladies so fine
So well to do
Looking serenely out at you
What was in their future... who knew?
They said there would soon be a war
Over by Christmas 1914 they foresaw

But now

Before anything had happened
They went to the photographic studio
In their Sunday best
Posing so formally
So their unity would be
Remembered for all time
Their youth and beauty would be preserved
Such splendid dresses
Meticulous hair
And such distinctive
And refined
Jewellery
What a day!
Life was for them and theirs
They lived and loved
Married, gave birth, grew old
And died

I suppose

Happiness and tragedy were theirs
Two World wars
A way of life disappeared

And then

They were forgotten
As if they never were
Someone's great great grandmothers

And the photograph so carefully posed for?

I found it for a pound in a charity shop ⚹

The Statue

The statue came alive
She did stretch and did writhe
In the warm morning's sun
Which with the new day had come
She felt the texture of her skin
And hoped that a new life did begin
She was pure, without sin
Her mind was in a spin
She stepped out of the pool
Through waters so cool
So perfect was she
Not like flawed humanity

She looked back at her plinth so bare
She had for centuries stood there
Alone in the centre of the park
In daylight and through the dark
Her arms had been raised at that site
Now she waved them and danced in delight

After a while she stood still
Found she was tired, with little will
To move, so she laid down and slept
Over her features the porcelain crept
The park keepers found her that day
On the grass as she lay
'Bloody vandals shifted her here
But she's still perfect, no wear'

The memories of her dance
Did her forever entrance ⁄⁄

Into the Light

She would soon be 85
Blessed with a long life
She lay there, wondering
How much longer
She had now, she had had enough

She remembered her mother
In the years before school, so long ago
Her children themselves
Were now old, those that still lived
Strange, and somehow wrong
To survive one of your children
Adolescence, boys
Discovering her body, her sexuality
Love, loss, joy and despair
Adventure and travel
Roaming the world
She was blessed with wealth and health
Until her body got tired, and started wearing out

She had fought, oh so hard
And kept going
After many operations
And treatments, and therapies
And drugs

But things got so hard
And now she could not travel
And her children had their lives
Far away and had to visit
When they could
So now eyesight and hearing, mobility
And so much worse were failing her
She no longer loved her life
Did not enjoy every day
Got the thrills, the pleasure

So now it was time to go
She relaxed and let go
And drifted away
Into the light

And was at rest ⁄⁄

His Choice

The kettle boiled
In the three minutes since he had filled it
And switched it on, his life had changed
In fact ended
He was shattered, he was giving up
The phone had rung, he answered it
And a voice, a remote anonymous voice
Ended his being
His wife, his beloved wife was dead

He sat still, numb, he did not want to cope
He did not want to live
He sat there and let go, he drifted
Felt his spirit leave his body and wander
Was this the afterlife? He felt easier
Not faced with survival, fighting to exist
He felt at peace
Then he hit a wall, well not a wall
Something, not solid
A force, a force with rage

He did not hear her, he felt her
She was in his mind
Calling him a selfish bastard
A coward, taking the easy way out
It was his wife, not in body but in spirit. She raged
Told him how their children would suffer
Two deaths at once
She had no choice, he did

Grandchildren deprived of their Grandma
Would lose a Grandad too
Selfish, selfish bastard
He felt her anger like physical blows
Forcing him back, back to his body
Making him live, making him go on.

He opened his eyes
Tears streamed down his cheeks
Sighed, stood up and made a cup of tea
Added sugar, a lot of sugar and drank deep ⁄⁄

Inspired by the opening words of a Roy Harper song sung by friend Katie Spencer

The House

It was magnificent, such a great new house
Large, roomy, she could have her family here
They would grow, live and love, like in a novel
Large gardens around it, secure with hedges
In the countryside, a hamlet, remote
Safe, a long happy life ahead
She was only thirty, she smiled
They moved in, decorated
Gardened, she gave birth
Several times
Were happy, loved and laughed
Middle age arrived, her kids left home
The house seemed large but they loved it still

Then she was alone
Her beloved husband died
The house was now vast
But she loved it still
Wanted to live out her days
Got help in to clean, the garden too
All was fine, she had been here 50 years
A lifetime
Then things went wrong
Her memory failed
She fell, repeatedly
No one moved back in to help
She was alone and struggled
The kids arranged her a place
A place in a home
There she lived out her days
Days with occasional, increasingly rare visits
No remote countryside now, no rolling fields
No quiet hamlet with a rosy future

The house would be sold when she died
Her son drove by for memory's sake

Was horrified
Dilapidated, neglected, sad overgrown
Like a gothic mansion in a horror film
Sinister, not happy
The cycle of her life ⫽

Lump

Lost weight, deliberately
A lot of weight, pleased
Place hand on my chest
Find lump, feel scared
Fright, dread, start to panic
As I do
Then
Am told by wife
That this is my breast bone
I should feel it, I used to feel it
Decades ago
Relief and feel very silly ⫽

Dark Bedroom

In a strange hotel
In middle of night
Get out of bed in darkness
Walk round bed
Fall over shoes, stub toe
Think 'Bloody Eileen'
Carelessly leaving shoes
Lying around
Turn on light in loo
See by light shoes are mine
Hurriedly put shoes away ⫽

Rock Climb

A friend took me to Derbyshire
To climb vast tall rock feature
Called a chimney
Near the top, paused
Thought
'Why am I here
How can I be scared and bored
At same time?'
Never climbed such a structure again ⁄⁄

Safe and Sound

Returned from dangerous
Rock climbing
Before mobiles invented
Went to fiancé's house
To reassure her I am ok
Her sister answers door
Can tell something up
Eileen sat in lounge
Looking abashed, arm in plaster
Fell on way to work, tripped over paving stone
That was sticking up
Hospital job, broke finger
Yet I am ok ⁄⁄

No Boundaries

Young man came in
Sat down with beer
Very tall, thin, dark skinned
With huge thick halo of hair

Woman at table in front
Turned, gawped, stared
Came over asked him
If the hair was all his
Natural, his own

He nodded, she leaned over
And with her hand
Grabbed his hair
Shook it firmly
He looked
Incredulous, aghast, invaded
She let go, odded
Now believed him
But had no idea she had crossed
A line, a boundary ⫽

Explosion Inside

Love, intense
Its hurts, physically inside me
Joy, disbelief
Exhilarated, yet stunned
I drive there amazed in wonderland
The smells of the hospital
My daughter in bed
The scent of milk
The sight, the silky hair
And the warmth in my arms
The blue eyed, tiny
Delicate baby
The wonder that is
My new born granddaughter ⫽

Seeing For Miles

Two lads, teenagers
Went to the fair
On the Stray in Harrogate
So much laughter
Fun on the big wheel
They saw for miles
Time passed
Friendship true and loving endured
As old men
They went to the seaside, Bridlington
One with a new hip
Saw the big wheel
Thought 'why not be daft?'

Two old men back up in the air
Laughter and fun
Again they saw for miles ⁄⁄

It's Not Fair

Went shopping in Asda
Bought a punnet of peaches
Stood in the queue thinking of how
I had been good and not
Bought bad, sweet or sugary stuff
Nothing with fat in that day

In front of me
A slim, oh so slim, man
About ten years younger than me
Then I saw his shopping
Oh it's not fair
How can it be fair?
How?

Chocolate!!
Six multi packs of Penguins and the like
Lard, Yes! Lard! Two blocks
A bottle of whiskey
16 cans of beer
And a huge tray of liver
Presumably to fry?

Yes a THIN man bought this lot
A very thin man
Oh it's not fair
Really it's not fair! ⁄⁄

It's Happened

When?
It's got here! When? And how?
A young pretty blond girl
Seated on a bus, she smiled
At me
I was flattered and pleased
She stood up
Gave up her seat
To the old guy
ME!

It's happened
How?
When?
Why?

And then it happened
Again
And again
And again ⁄⁄

Other anthologies and collections available from Stairwell Books

For further information please contact rose@stairwellbooks.com
www.stairwellbooks.co.uk
@stairwellbooks

Lightning Source UK Ltd.
Milton Keynes UK
UKHW010941120221
378674UK00001B/61